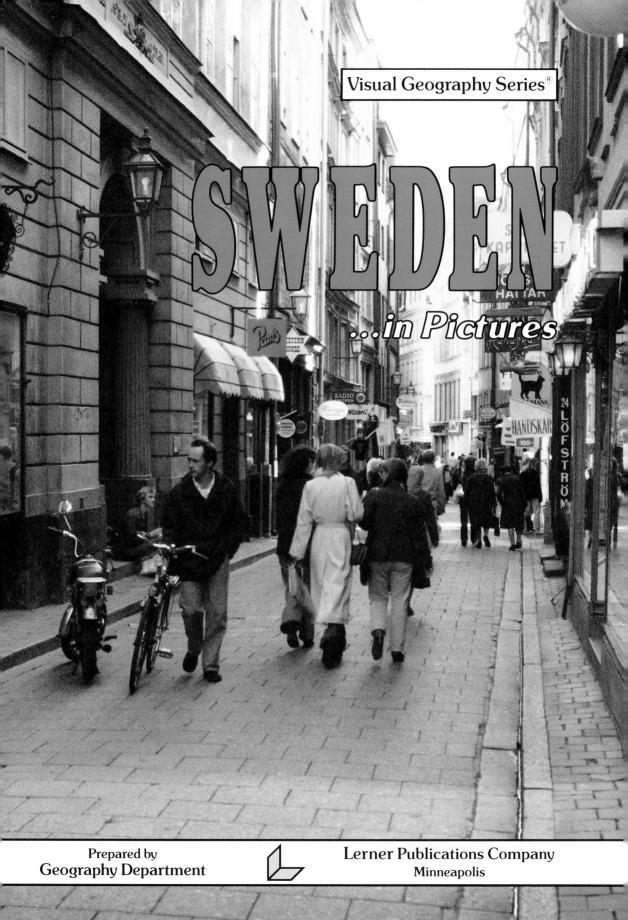

Visual Geography Series®

SWEDEN

...in Pictures

Prepared by
Geography Department

Lerner Publications Company
Minneapolis

Courtesy of John Rice

Although they are primarily city dwellers, many Swedes like to spend their weekends in rural areas.

This book is an all-new edition in the Visual Geography Series. Previous editions were published by Sterling Publishing Company, New York City. The text, set in 10/12 Century Textbook, is fully revised and updated, and new photographs, maps, charts, and captions have been added.

Website address: www.lernerbooks.com

LIBRARY OF CONGRESS CATALOGING-IN-PUBLICATION DATA

Sweden in pictures / prepared by Geography Department, Lerner Publications Company.
  p.   cm. — (Visual geography series)
  Rev. ed. of: Sweden in pictures / prepared by Jo McDonald.
  Includes bibliographical references.
  Summary: Text and photographs introduce Sweden's history, geography, economy, people, and government.
  ISBN 0–8225–1872–4
  1. Sweden. [1. Sweden] I. McDonald, Jo. Sweden in pictures. II. Lerner Publications Company. Geography Dept.   III. Series: Visual geography series (Minneapolis, Minn.)
DL609.S94   1990
948.5—dc20   90–34974
                                          CIP
                                          AC

International Standard Book Number: 0–8225–1824–4
Library of Congress Catalog Card Number: 90–34974

VISUAL GEOGRAPHY SERIES®

Publisher
Harry Jonas Lerner
Associate Publisher
Nancy M. Campbell
Senior Editor
Mary M. Rodgers
Editors
Gretchen Bratvold
Dan Filbin
Phyllis Schuster
Photo Researcher
Kerstin Coyle
Editorial/Photo Assistant
Marybeth Campbell
Consultants/Contributors
John G. Rice
Sandra K. Davis
Designer
Jim Simondet
Cartographer
Carol F. Barrett
Indexers
Kristine S. Schubert
Sylvia Timian
Production Manager
Gary J. Hansen

Courtesy of Swedish Tourist Board

Many windmills, used now for storage, mark the landscape of Öland, an island off Sweden's eastern coast.

Acknowledgments

Title page photo courtesy of Harlan V. Anderson.

Elevation contours adapted from *The Times Atlas of the World,* seventh comprehensive edition (New York: Times Books, 1985).

Three vowels that appear at the end of the Swedish alphabet are used in this book. The letter "å" often sounds like a long "o" in English, and the "ä" like a short "e," as in step. The "ö" is pronounced "eu," as in adieu.

3   4   5   6   7   8   –   JR   –   03   02   01   00   99   98

The City Hall in Stockholm, the capital of Sweden, was completed in 1927. The red brick building serves as a backdrop for Sailboat Day, an annual event on Lake Mälar.

Contents

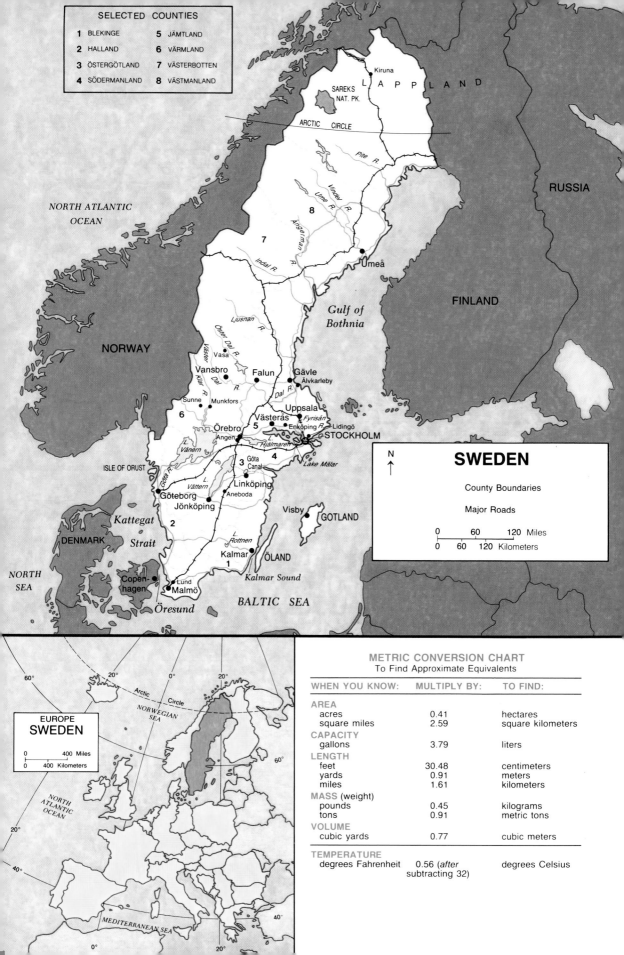

SELECTED COUNTIES

1 BLEKINGE   5 JÄMTLAND
2 HALLAND   6 VÄRMLAND
3 ÖSTERGÖTLAND   7 VÄSTERBOTTEN
4 SÖDERMANLAND   8 VÄSTMANLAND

L A P P L A N D

Kiruna

SAREKS NAT. PK.

ARCTIC CIRCLE

Pite R.

RUSSIA

NORTH ATLANTIC OCEAN

Vindel R.

Ume R.

8

Ångerman R.

7

Indal R.

Umeå

FINLAND

Gulf of Bothnia

NORWAY

Ljusnan R.

Öster Dal R.

Väster Dal R.

Vasa

Vansbro

Falun

Gävle

Klar R.

Älvkarleby

Dal R.

Sunne

Munkfors

Uppsala

6

Örebro

Västerås

Fyrisån

Enköping R.

Lidingö

Angen

5

STOCKHOLM

L. Vänern

Hjälmaren

4

Lake Mälar

N

SWEDEN

County Boundaries

Major Roads

ISLE OF ORUST

Göta R.

3

Göta Canal

L. Vättern

Linköping

Aneboda

Göteborg

Jönköping

Visby

GOTLAND

0   60   120 Miles
0   60   120 Kilometers

Kattegat

DENMARK

Strait

2

L. Rottnen

ÖLAND

Kalmar

1

NORTH SEA

Copen-hagen

Lund

Malmö

Öresund

Kalmar Sound

BALTIC SEA

60°

20°

0°

20°

Arctic Circle

NORWEGIAN SEA

EUROPE
SWEDEN

0   400 Miles
0   400 Kilometers

60°

NORTH ATLANTIC OCEAN

20°

40°

MEDITERRANEAN SEA

0°

20°

40°

METRIC CONVERSION CHART
To Find Approximate Equivalents

WHEN YOU KNOW:	MULTIPLY BY:	TO FIND:
AREA		
acres	0.41	hectares
square miles	2.59	square kilometers
CAPACITY		
gallons	3.79	liters
LENGTH		
feet	30.48	centimeters
yards	0.91	meters
miles	1.61	kilometers
MASS (weight)		
pounds	0.45	kilograms
tons	0.91	metric tons
VOLUME		
cubic yards	0.77	cubic meters
TEMPERATURE		
degrees Fahrenheit	0.56 (*after* subtracting 32)	degrees Celsius

Hills fringed with evergreens and dotted with red farm buildings are typical of many parts of Sweden. This countryside is near Angen in the Värmland region.

Introduction

The Kingdom of Sweden is a democratic nation in Scandinavia—a northern European region that includes Norway, Denmark, and, for some geographers, Finland and Iceland. Sweden's 8.9 million people enjoy a high standard of living and considerable economic security. They live in a welfare state—a country in which the government assumes responsibility for the well-being of its people. To fund government services, Swedes pay high taxes.

Sweden has a long history of political freedom. In ancient times, most people were free farmers, or peasants, who lived in largely independent provinces headed by a local leader or king. Unwritten laws protected the people's rights. From about A.D. 750 to 1000, most parts of Sweden came under the control of the Svear king, who ruled from Uppland. Through assemblies in each province, the people had a say in how they were governed and even in who the Swedish ruler would be.

While Sweden was uniting internally, fleets of Swedish Vikings sailed to eastern Europe, first on raids but later on trading expeditions. In the 1200s, German merchants began to establish commercial centers on Swedish soil. The Germans were attracted by Sweden's minerals and forests—the basis of the country's natural wealth. The 1500s and 1600s were centuries of territorial growth for Sweden, which fought many wars with Russia, Poland, and Denmark. A serious defeat by Russia in 1709 ended Swedish expansion, and by the early 1800s the country had lost most of its European possessions.

In the following decades, economic hardships caused thousands of Swedes to emigrate to the United States. By the end of the nineteenth century, emigration slowed as industrialization created more jobs in Sweden. A socialist political party—the Social Democrats—had also organized.

The party's philosophy of sharing the national wealth to create a better life for all citizens became popular among Swedes. Modern Sweden's success—under the leadership of the Social Democrats—was achieved through widespread cooperation among its citizens.

Throughout the twentieth century, Sweden has followed a policy of neutrality—or "not taking sides"—in its dealings with other nations. For this reason, the country did not participate in World Wars I or II. Sweden takes an active role in assisting developing countries and in supporting programs that promote world peace.

Sweden looks after the needs of its citizens from birth to old age. Most Swedes retire at age 65. Government pensions provide retirees *(right)* with an income equal to about two-thirds of the wages they received while employed. Day-care workers *(below)* watch over many Swedish children in government-sponsored nurseries that meet the needs of working parents.

Courtesy of Chad Ehlers

Courtesy of Chad Ehlers

A light snow covers a farm in southwestern Lappland, as well as the peaks of the Kölen Mountains. Lappland, Sweden's northernmost region, has a long winter and a very short summer.

1) The Land

Sweden, a sparsely populated country, occupies the eastern part of the Scandinavian Peninsula. With 174,000 square miles, Sweden is Europe's fourth largest country. It is slightly bigger than the state of California, stretching almost 1,000 miles from north to south. The Arctic Circle runs through Lappland, the country's northernmost region.

North-south mountain ranges form most of the 1,000-mile western border between Sweden and Norway. In the northeast, the country shares a 360-mile boundary with Finland. Most of eastern Sweden is bounded by the Baltic Sea. The Gulf of Bothnia is the arm of the Baltic that separates Sweden and Finland. A narrow channel of water called the Öresund connects the North Sea to the Baltic Sea.

Topography

Most of Sweden is less than 1,000 feet above sea level. Elevations are highest in northern Sweden's Kölen Mountains. The flattest, lowest plains are in the far south.

Farm buildings in Skåne, Sweden's most fertile agricultural area, glisten in the sun after a summer shower. Farmers dry hay by hanging it over racks in their fields.

The ice that covered Scandinavia during the last Ice Age helped shape Sweden's topography. The covering was so heavy that it pushed the earth's crust down, and the land is still rising as it regains its former elevation. Individual glaciers (ice masses) broadened river valleys and carved lakes in northern Sweden.

SOUTHERN AND CENTRAL SWEDEN

Southern Sweden, which is sometimes called Götaland, has several distinct topographical features. A large area of fertile plains occupies the extreme southern tip of the region, which is called Skåne or Scania. These plains are a continuation of the flatlands of Denmark and northern

An archipelago (group of islands) off Sweden's western coast is located near one of the world's finest fishing grounds. Many of the rocky islands are barren of vegetation.

Germany. Land now covered by sea once connected those countries to Sweden.

The Småland region begins just north of Scania. Heavily wooded highlands cover much of Småland. Soils are less fertile in these highlands, where forestry is an important activity. The narrow coastal island of Öland, which is about 70 miles long, lies east of Småland. Göteborg and Malmö, the country's second and third largest cities, are situated on the western coast of southern Sweden.

North of the highlands—in Svealand, which means "land of the Swedes"—are lakes, plains, and rolling hills. Svealand lies in the southern half of the country but is called central Sweden. It includes the areas of Södermanland, Östergötland, Närke, Värmland, Västmanland, Dalarna, Gästrikland, and Uppland. Near the eastern coast of Svealand lies Stockholm,

Sweden's capital and biggest city. The large Baltic island of Gotland is also considered a part of central Sweden.

NORTHERN SWEDEN

The northern three-fifths of Sweden—Norrland—contains mountains, high plateaus, rolling hills, broad river valleys, and a narrow coastal plain. Skerries (rock islets) dot the shoreline on the Gulf of Bothnia. Except in river valleys, the soil in Norrland is poor, and most of the region is forested. The high elevations of western Norrland reach above the timberline (the height beyond which trees will not grow).

Mountains extend through western Norrland. The ranges rise to their greatest heights on Norway's side of the border, but many peaks jut above Sweden's high plateaus as well. The tallest are Mount Kebnekaise (6,965 feet) and Mount Sarektjåkkå (6,857 feet), which are in Lappland. Many rivers flow from Norrland's mountains, widening in some parts into long, narrow lakes.

Along the eastern side of the mountains, rolling hills form a band that varies from 90 to 150 miles in width. Forests, interrupted by marshes and peat bogs (which form wet, spongy ground), cover the region. These uplands decrease in elevation from about 2,000 feet near the mountains to 650 feet at the Gulf of Bothnia. The northern third of Norrland extends north of the Arctic Circle and is known as the Land of the Midnight Sun. For almost two months in summer, daylight lasts con-

Courtesy of Herbert Fristedt

Sweden's topography varies from intensively cultivated flat land in the south *(left)* to untouched wilderness in the far north *(below)*. Sarek National Park in northern Sweden is the largest wilderness area in Europe. It has 100 glaciers (slow-moving ice masses) but no trails, cabins, or bridges. The park can only be seen on foot, and hunting and fishing are prohibited. The Swedish people have decided not to develop Sarek's land and rivers.

Courtesy of Chad Ehlers

Sweden has about 100,000 lakes. Stockholm sits on 14 islands at the eastern edge of Lake Mälar, the country's third largest lake. The long body of water extends westward for 73 miles. Lake Mälar was an arm of the Baltic Sea until the twelfth century, when falling water levels created an inland lake. Many castles and estates are situated on the lake's shores.

tinuously there. For the same length of time in winter, the region experiences twilight and darkness.

Lakes and Rivers

Sweden contains about 100,000 lakes, whose combined area represents 8.6 percent of the country's surface. Central Sweden's Lake Vänern, the biggest lake in western Europe, is so vast that it resembles an inland sea. Lakes Vättern, Mälar, and Hjälmaren in the southern half of the country are also very large.

To create a water-transportation route from the Baltic to Göteborg, Swedish engineers completed the Göta Canal in 1832. An important waterway for many decades, the route passes through Lake Vänern, Lake Vättern, and several other lakes. The 55-mile canal contains 65 locks—chambers that raise and lower boats by adjusting water levels. Modern tourists use the canal to see central Sweden.

A passenger boat crosses central Sweden on the Göta Canal, which links the Baltic Sea and the Kattegat Strait.

Sweden's rivers have been very important to the country's economy. Water power was a key resource for industrialization. By the late 1800s, the power of flowing rivers was being converted to electricity and transmitted to cities. Although most logs are transported on land, rivers once provided a practical way for foresters to move timber to the sea.

Norrland's rivers run in a southeasterly direction from the mountains to the Gulf of Bothnia. The waterways descend gradually and contain few high waterfalls that can provide electric power. Swedish engineers, therefore, have designed vertical tunnels at the top of some rapids to capture water and make it fall straight down, producing greater force. The water then runs through a horizontal tunnel to rejoin the river below the rapids.

Sweden's longest river, the Dal, is formed where the Väster Dal River joins the Öster Dal River. The waterway then follows a 250-mile course to enter the Baltic at Gävle, about 90 miles north of Stockholm.

Northward from that point, many rivers empty into the Baltic. These northern waterways—each of which is more than 200 miles long—include the Ljusnan, the Indal, the Ångerman, the Ume, the Vindel, and the Pite.

A major river of central Sweden, the Klar, begins in Norway and flows 250 miles southward into Lake Vänern. The Göta River emerges from the lake's southern end and enters the Kattegat Strait at Göteborg.

Climate

Although Sweden is situated in the far north, the warm North Atlantic Current, which affects weather on the Scandinavian Peninsula, moderates the country's climate. Southwesterly winds blowing from the Atlantic bring warmth and short periods of rain. At times, air masses from the European continent push into Sweden. These air masses produce hot, dry spells in summer and cold, dry weather in winter.

Courtesy of Harlan V. Anderson

A power plant harnesses the energy of the Dal River at Älvkarleby in central Sweden. Workers constructed the country's first hydroelectric stations in the late 1800s. Such installations now provide 50 percent of Sweden's electrical energy.

Before hydroelectric facilities were built on many rivers, foresters used the waterways for transporting logs. The Klar *(above)* is one of the last Swedish rivers on which log floating still occurs.

In summer, northern and southern Sweden experience similar temperatures. Norrland stays warm because of its longer hours of daylight. North of the Arctic Circle, the sun shines for 24 hours a day in midsummer. Even areas as far south as Stockholm, however, experience only a few hours of darkness on June nights.

Winter brings greater temperature differences between northern and southern regions. The average temperature in Kiruna, which is north of the Arctic Circle, is 9° F in February (Sweden's coldest month) and 55° F in July (the hottest month). Corresponding readings in Stockholm are 26° and 64° F. In Malmö—the southernmost large city—temperatures average 31° F in February and 63° F in July.

Most parts of Sweden receive 20 to 30 inches of rainfall annually, but the western mountains and the southern highlands usually record more than 30 inches. The extreme north gets less than 20 inches of precipitation each year. Southern Sweden typically receives snow in January and February, but the north is snow-covered for six months. The Gulf of Bothnia usually freezes in the winter, closing ports north of Stockholm by mid-January.

Flora and Fauna

Evergreen forests of spruce and Scotch pine cover much of Sweden. On the higher slopes, evergreens give way to birch forests. Hardy shrubs, grasses, and meadow

Värmland experiences late twilights during summertime. At Lake Rottnen, the sun still colors the sky at 11:30 P.M.

Forests cover more than 50 percent of Sweden. The national or local governments own one-fourth of the forested land. Another one-fourth belongs to timber companies, and other private owners hold title to the rest.

vegetation replace forests at elevations above the timberline in the far north. Still higher, buttercups, mosses, and lichens cover soil and rocks. At the highest alpine elevations, no vegetation is able to grow.

In the forests of central Sweden, birch, aspen, and mountain ash are scattered among the evergreens. Beech and oak forests once crowded the southern coast of Sweden but were long ago cleared for farming. However, those and other hardwoods—including ash, elm, maple, and linden—still thrive in the remaining wooded areas of southern and central Sweden. Many varieties of flowering plants—including orchids and rockroses—grow wild on the islands of Öland and Gotland and in eastern Skåne.

Many species of berry-producing shrubs cover forest floors. Outdoor enthusiasts can find many berries, including lingonberries, cloudberries, raspberries, and strawberries, growing wild in the countryside. An old tradition allows anyone—without asking permission—to enter forests and fields to pick mushrooms and berries. As a result, most privately held rural land is available for the public to enjoy, providing the visitors do not harm the property.

A family picks wild berries in southern Sweden. An ancient right of common use allows anyone to wander freely in woods, meadows, and fields and to collect wild berries, mushrooms, and most wildflowers.

Sweden has large populations of moose and roe deer. Each year during hunting season, hunters shoot about 100,000 moose, but the animals still number more than 350,000. Hares, foxes, ermines, weasels, red squirrels, and elks are also found throughout Sweden. Three carnivores (meat-eaters) of the northern forests—bears, wolverines, and lynxes—are now rarely seen, and wolves are almost extinct in Sweden.

Lemmings (small plant-eating members of the mouse family) and arctic foxes live in the northern highlands. Wild reindeer no longer exist, but Lapps keep large domesticated herds. Sweden has few reptiles or amphibians and has only one poisonous snake—the viper. Insects are common throughout the country. One of the most annoying—the gadfly—attacks reindeer in the spring, causing so much discomfort that the animals leave their winter pastures in the forests for grazing lands on the high plains.

Spring brings many species of migratory birds to Sweden. Teal and wagtail ducks, snipes, and golden plovers are among the most numerous. Coastal birds include gulls, terns, eider ducks (whose down is prized

Independent Picture Service

The bullfinch is often seen in city parks as well as in the woods of Sweden. The male bird has a brilliant red breast, a gray back, and a white rump.The wing tips and head are black.

for bedding), and rare sea eagles. The ptarmigan inhabits mountains of the north. Elsewhere, grouse, cranes, and partridges are found. Sweden's lakes and rivers contain salmon, trout, pike, and perch. The North Sea yields cod, mackerel, herring, and flatfish. The Baltic provides great hauls of strömming, a small herring.

Courtesy of Swedish Tourist Board

About 2,500 of the 17,000 Lapps living in Sweden partly depend on the herding of reindeer for their livelihood. The animals—raised mainly for meat—graze in large herds.

15

Fires destroyed Stockholm's original wooden houses. Citizens replaced them with substantial stone buildings. Many water channels enhance the city's beauty.

Major Cities

More than 1.5 million people live in Stockholm, Sweden's capital, largest city, commercial center, and financial hub. Stockholm sprawls over 14 islands at the eastern end of Lake Mälar, near the Baltic Sea. One-third of the city's area is parkland. On the Baltic coast east of Stockholm is an archipelago of 24,000 islands, many of which lie between the city and the open waters of the sea.

The city was founded in the thirteenth century, and by the fifteenth century it had become the political center of the country. The Royal Palace in Stockholm is the largest royal residence still in use in Europe. The city's museums include the Medieval Museum, which depicts Stockholm's origins and history, and the Historical Museum, which displays the region's Viking heritage.

With a population of 705,000, Göteborg (or Gothenburg) is Sweden's second largest urban area. Situated at the mouth of the Göta River on the Kattegat Strait, the city is a major port and manufacturing hub.

Trolley cars roll by restaurants, night-clubs, and shops on a main thorough-fare in Göteborg, Sweden's second largest urban area. One of the most popular attractions in this seaport city is Liseberg, Sweden's biggest amusement park.

The automotive and aerospace industries are important to the city's economy. Founded in 1619 by the Swedish king Gustavus Adolphus, Göteborg was designed by Dutch architects who patterned the town after Amsterdam, the capital of the Netherlands.

Malmö (population 460,000) is the main urban center of southern Sweden. Although the city was founded in the thirteenth cen-tury, its site has been inhabited since at least 8000 B.C. Malmö is only 40 minutes by hydrofoil from Copenhagen, Denmark, and until 1658 it was a Danish city. In that year, the Swedish king Karl X brought it under Swedish control. An important port, Malmö exports grain, sugar, cement, and clay. The city is also a center for ship-building, food processing, textile manufac-turing, and railway-car production.

Malmö, Sweden's third largest city, can trace its origins to the thirteenth century, when the southernmost regions of Sweden were part of Denmark. A harbor built in the 1700s made Malmö a major port.

Secondary Urban Areas

Four other Swedish cities have populations of more than 100,000. The historic city of Uppsala (population 146,000) is situated in the area that was settled by the Svear—the people who dominated the country by A.D. 1000. Uppsala became the center for the Christian religion in Sweden in 1164. The University of Uppsala, Sweden's oldest institution of higher learning, was established in 1477. Modern-day Uppsala supports a variety of industries, including engineered products, pharmaceuticals, and printing.

Situated on Lake Mälar, Västerås (population 118,000) is a major inland port from which lumber, iron ore, and iron products are shipped. The city is also a center of the Swedish electrical industry. A castle built in the 1200s dominates the city's center, and burial mounds dating from Viking times are nearby.

Linköping, in southeastern Sweden, has 113,000 people. This ancient settlement became a Catholic bishop's see (seat of power) in 1100. Aircraft and automobile manufacturing are important to the city's economy. Jönköping, with 108,000 people, was established in 1284 at the southern end of Lake Vättern. The city was destroyed and rebuilt in the 1600s. It produces matches, airplanes, paper, and machinery.

Courtesy of John Rice

The Fyrisån River flows through Uppsala in the area of Uppland. Kings of the Svear people, who lived in Uppland, controlled most of Sweden by A.D. 1000. In 1272 Uppsala became the see (seat of power) of the Roman Catholic archbishop, the top church official in Sweden at that time. Sweden's first university was established in the city in 1477.

Early in its history, Sweden developed a network of small kingdoms that eventually formed one realm. Gustav Vasa, one of the country's most able monarchs, led Swedes in a successful revolt against Danish control. In 1523 he was elected king, becoming the first ruler in the House of Vasa. His statue is at the Nordic Museum in Stockholm.

Courtesy of Harlan V. Anderson

2) History and Government

About 12,000 B.C., near the end of the last Ice Age, the Scandinavian Peninsula began to emerge from a thick ice cap. As the ice retreated, groups of hunters and gatherers of Germanic stock moved northward into Sweden. Archaeologists have found evidence of human habitation in southern Sweden that dates from about 10,000 B.C.

By 2500 B.C., later migrants who knew how to farm had settled in southern Sweden. They raised grain and cattle. Scientific findings indicate that a third migration into Sweden probably had occurred by 1500 B.C. Called boat-axe peoples after the shape of their stone axes, these groups probably crossed the Baltic Sea from Finland.

Containers, ornaments, and weapons from the period show that by 1500 B.C. the people in Sweden were skilled in working bronze and copper. Swedish traders sailed to ports in Europe, exchanging furs, amber (fossilized tree resin), and possibly slaves for iron weapons, salt, and jewelry.

The 5,000-year-old stone tomb called Hagerdösen stands north of Göteborg on the Isle of Orust.

Historians believe that a severe climatic change disrupted trade after 500 B.C. and that commerce with the outer world did not resume until 100 B.C.

By that time, the Götar—a Germanic people related to the Goths—had developed a strong kingdom in southern Sweden. In A.D. 400, the Götar traveled as far as the Black Sea, making contact with the Eastern and Western Roman empires. On their return, the Götar brought back knowledge of writing to Sweden.

Another powerful kingdom, that of the Svear, had developed farther north around Lake Mälar. From their center near modern-day Uppsala, Svear kings gradually extended their influence over other areas of Sweden. Sometime between A.D. 750 and 1000, the Svear gained control of the provinces of the Götar. Sweden derives its name (*Sverige*, in Swedish) from the Svear.

Runestones *(middle and bottom)*—rocks that carry markings in the ancient rune alphabet—are scattered throughout Scandinavia, a region that includes Sweden, Norway, and Denmark. Sweden's 3,000 runestones record some of the country's early history, including the activities of Swedish Vikings. These pirates and traders carved such stones to preserve their deeds for future generations. Some runic symbols appear on grave markers.

The Viking Era

From 800 to 1050, sailors from provinces in Sweden, Norway, and Denmark journeyed abroad to acquire foreign goods and territories. The Scandinavians of this period later became known as Vikings. The term may have come from *vik,* the Norse word for "fjord" or "bay."

Traveling in long, swift boats, the early Vikings carried out surprise attacks and destructive raids on European ports. These acts gave the Scandinavian sailors a reputation as pirates. Gradually, however, Viking expeditions became larger and better organized, with armies and navies under the command of chieftains. Peaceful trading replaced the looting and burning of earlier expeditions.

The Vikings of Denmark and southwestern Sweden voyaged southward, and the Norwegian Vikings crossed the Atlantic to Iceland and Greenland. Vikings from eastern Sweden sailed to ports on the Baltic Sea. Using rivers that reached far into what is now Russia, the Swedish Vikings established short-lived kingdoms. These sailors also journeyed to the Black and Caspian seas, exchanging furs and forest products for goods from realms farther east.

The origins of democracy in Sweden go back at least to the Viking era. Although

This replica is similar to ships that Scandinavian Vikings used 1,000 years ago. Swedish Vikings (also known as Varangians) used the vessels to cross the Baltic Sea and to sail down rivers into northern Europe. The Swedish adventurers established kingdoms at Novgorod in Russia and Kiev in Ukraine. Some historians believe that the people who lived in the area called the newcomers "Rus" and that from this term the name Russia was eventually derived.

wealthier classes were emerging, peasants formed the bulk of the population. In Sweden, the peasant class consisted mainly of farmers and foresters who worked small plots of land. These minor landholders were accustomed to much personal freedom. In most provinces, peasants were represented in an assembly, called the *ting,* that enforced local laws. Socially, women were nearly equal to men and ran the farms when Viking men were away on voyages.

Christianity reached Sweden in the early 800s, when Ansgar, a missionary born in Rheims, France, traveled to the country and converted some of its inhabitants. Nevertheless, most Swedish people continued to worship several gods throughout much of the Viking era. The main deities were Odin (god of wisdom), Frey (god of fertility), and Thor (god of strength). This traditional religion was not organized, and different regions observed different customs. Some practices involved human and animal sacrifices to bring good fortune. By telling stories, people passed down

tales of the gods and of elves, trolls, and giants. By the end of the Viking era, however, Christianity was becoming widely accepted.

Expansion to Finland

In the 1100s, most provinces of Sweden governed themselves, although they paid taxes and pledged loyalty to the king in Uppsala. In 1150 King Erik IX ruled in Uppsala. To stop invasions by the Finns, Erik led an expedition into southwestern Finland and established some Swedish control in that area. From 1160 to 1250, two rival families—the Sverker and the Erik—alternately held the crown. The struggles between the two families weakened the monarchy and increased the power of the *jarl,* an administrator whose role was second only to that of the king.

The jarl's power had developed during the Viking age, when the king gave him the authority to assemble a great fleet, or *ledung,* for an expedition. In order to get

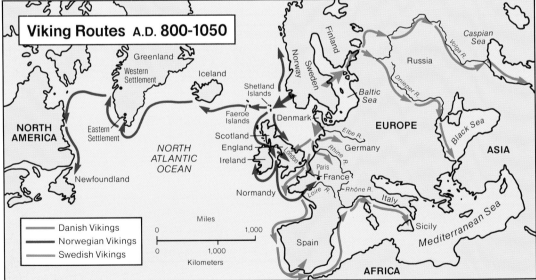

Artwork by Laura Westlund

Between A.D. 800 and 1050, the height of the Viking era, Scandinavians sailed in three main directions to plunder, trade, and settle other regions. Most Swedes traveled to eastern Europe. The Danes went south, raiding Germany, France, the British Isles, Spain, and the Mediterranean coast. The Norwegians focused most of their attention westward, on Iceland, Greenland, and North America.

Kalmar Castle, in the Småland region of southern Sweden, sits on Kalmar Sound, facing the island of Öland. The oldest parts of the five-towered structure date to the early eleventh century. The castle was enlarged in the sixteenth century. It was besieged many times, particularly by Danish forces when Denmark and Sweden battled for control of lands around the Baltic Sea in the sixteenth and seventeenth centuries.

Photo by Robert Paulson

enough ships, provinces were divided into districts called *hundreds*. The jarl required most of the hundreds, when summoned, to provide two ships and crews to sail them. The ledung continued to serve Sweden as a military force after the Viking era ended. During the thirteenth century, however, Sweden came to rely on armed knights for defense. The wealthy families that provided the knights became the Swedish aristocracy.

By 1250 Sweden controlled the southwestern parts of Finland and had established the city of Visby, on the island of Gotland, as a trading and military base. Some present-day areas of southwestern

A mosaic in Stockholm's City Hall depicts a Swedish knight of the Middle Ages (A.D. 500 to 1500). By the mid-thirteenth century, the mounted knight protected by armor had a definite advantage over soldiers on foot. Swedish kings encouraged landowners and officials to outfit themselves as knights. In return for military service, knights did not have to pay property taxes.

Courtesy of Harlan V. Anderson

23

Visby, on the Baltic island of Gotland, was one of Europe's main commercial centers from about 1100 to 1500. Many foreign merchants, especially Germans in the Hanseatic League, settled in the city. Long, thick walls were built around Visby in the 1200s to protect warehouses from thieves.

Courtesy of Swedish Tourist Board

Sweden, however, belonged at that time to Denmark or Norway.

The Folkung Dynasty

In 1250, when the last Erik king died, the jarl—whose name was Birger—persuaded the nobility to choose his own young son, Valdemar, as the next king. The dynasty (family of rulers) that Birger established became known as the Folkung dynasty. For the first 16 years of Folkung control, Birger Jarl guided Valdemar and was the actual ruler of Sweden.

The country prospered under Birger Jarl's administration. He issued the first national laws, which were designed to promote peace and order in Sweden. Persons who broke the laws could be banished from the realm. Daughters as well as sons received inheritance rights. Birger Jarl founded Stockholm and encouraged trade with the Hanseatic League, an association of trading towns based in Germany. Visby became a major center of the league.

Birger Jarl's policies were continued by his second son, Magnus Ladulås, who became king in 1275 after revolting against his brother Valdemar. Magnus allowed Ger-man merchants in the Hanseatic League to develop Sweden's copper resources at Falun. Although this stimulated Sweden's economy, the privileges and influence granted to the Germans at Falun and elsewhere angered many Swedes. Magnus also increased the power of the Roman Catholic Church by making all church lands free from taxation. A council of royal advisers became an important part of the government. The council consisted of legal experts, church leaders, and three governmental administrators.

In the early 1300s, Sweden was linked to Norway for the first time through the rule of another Folkung king, Magnus II Eriksson, who was also king of Norway. A weak monarch, Magnus II lost control of Norway in 1343 but continued to rule Sweden until 1360. Nevertheless, he was not strong enough to protect his realm from the growing power of Swedish nobles and from the economic influence of the German merchants. In addition, attempts by other countries to acquire Swedish territory threatened the kingdom.

Sweden was further weakened after 1350 by the spread of the bubonic plague, or Black Death, which disease-infested rats

A Swedish noblewoman named Birgitta had a strong influence on Sweden in the 1300s. Traveling in Europe, she studied the social and political problems people faced. Later, her activism and writings had a significant impact on the educated people of her day, including Sweden's rulers. Birgitta established an order of nuns and was later named a saint.

A modern statue by Carl Milles depicts Engelbrekt Engelbrektsson, leader of a peasant revolt against Danish rule in 1435.

carried throughout Europe. The epidemic killed one-third of the Swedish population. This loss, combined with the political instability of the period, brought about an economic decline that lasted through the 1400s.

The Union of Kalmar

Magnus's successor, a German named Albrekt of Mecklenburg, wanted to decrease the nobles' power, and he was soon at odds with the council of advisers. Albrekt appointed his German relatives to high offices and called in their army. To meet this threat, the council turned to Norway for support and elected Margrete, who ruled Norway and Denmark, to run Sweden's government. Margrete, who was born in Denmark, had succeeded her husband and her father to the Danish throne. Her forces captured Albrekt in 1389 and eventually drove the Mecklenburg family from Sweden. Intelligent and skillful, Margrete in 1397 formally united Sweden, Norway, and Denmark in the Union of Kalmar. Before she died in 1412, Margrete restricted the powers of the nobility.

Margrete's successor—her nephew, Erik of Pomerania—quickly lost the popular support Margrete had gained for the crown. As head of the Union of Kalmar, he thought primarily of Denmark's interests and taxed Swedish peasants heavily to fund Danish wars. He also angered the Hanseatic merchants by making their ships pay a toll. In response to Erik's policies, the Hanseatic League blockaded Sweden, preventing the country from obtaining a vital import—salt. Erik further reduced the nobles' authority, angering them as well.

In 1435 opposition by Swedish farmers and laborers led to Erik's overthrow and to Sweden's temporary withdrawal from the Union of Kalmar. In that year, Engelbrekt Engelbrektsson, a mine owner in Bergslagen, led a rebellion by miners and peasants. The protest was supported

Courtesy of Harlan V. Anderson

An artist in the 1400s painted murals on the ceiling of Härkeberga Church near Enköping. The murals depict the everyday life of people who lived at that time.

by Swedish nobles and spread rapidly throughout the country. Three months after the revolt began, Engelbrekt was installed as head of Sweden's government.

With Erik deposed, however, the nobility had no further use for Engelbrekt, and certain nobles arranged for his murder in 1436. For several years, the Swedish council controlled state affairs, but representatives of the peasantry began to attend state meetings. Out of these gatherings grew the Swedish *Riksdag,* or parliament. Represented in the new body were four estates (groups)—peasants, burghers (the middle class), nobles, and clergy.

The peasants' revolt of 1435 also strengthened Sweden's sense of national identity. In the following decades, groups that opposed the Union of Kalmar often determined who would rule Sweden. At times, Danish rulers attempted to reestablish their authority.

In 1520 the Danish ruler Christian II invaded Sweden. His large military force killed Sten Sture the Younger, who headed Sweden's government, and defeated the Swedish army. To overcome opposition to his rule, Christian later had his soldiers behead 82 leading noblemen in Stockholm's central square.

Gamla Stan, or Old Town, is one of the oldest parts of Stockholm. In 1520 Christian II, the king of Denmark, led his troops to Stockholm and massacred 82 leading citizens in Gamla Stan's main square.

Courtesy of Swedish Tourist Board

Courtesy of Harlan V. Anderson

A painting in Uppsala Cathedral shows people welcoming Gustavus Adolphus after a triumphant battle that expanded Sweden's territory in Europe. The king—who was the dominant figure in Sweden in the early 1600s—was killed during the Thirty Years' War (1618-1648).

The Vasa Kings

The massacre in Stockholm strengthened Swedish opposition to Danish rule. In 1521 Gustav Vasa, a young noble whose father was one of the 82 victims, organized a peasant uprising. Within two years, Gustav's forces drove the Danes from Sweden. The Riksdag elected Gustav king in 1523.

Gustav took measures to improve governmental efficiency and to stimulate mining, agriculture, and commerce. To increase the wealth and power of the state, he allowed the government to seize the property of the Roman Catholic Church, which owned one-fifth of the country's land. The Protestant Reformation—a religious reform movement—had spread to Sweden from central Europe. Gustav encouraged Protestantism, mainly to undermine the authority of the Roman Catholic Church. Through his efforts, a Protestant denomination—the Lutheran Church—became Sweden's official religious organization.

During Gustav Vasa's reign, the Riksdag made Sweden a hereditary monarchy. After Gustav died in 1560, several of his sons and grandsons inherited the crown. During the Vasa period, Sweden fought against Denmark, Poland, and Russia in an attempt to expand Swedish territory.

When Gustav Vasa's grandson Gustavus Adolphus came to the throne in 1611, Sweden was losing its wars of conquest. The new king, who was 17 when his reign began, concluded the wars with treaties and quickly displayed a capacity for leadership. Working with the skilled statesman Axel Oxenstierna, he reformed the central and local governments and the judiciary. Gustavus developed the country's mineral resources and encouraged foreign investment. The state overhauled its army and navy and improved the educational system.

In other parts of Europe—mainly Austria and Germany—the Hapsburg Empire was fighting to stamp out the growth of

Independent Picture Service

Gustavus Adolphus, king of Sweden from 1611 to 1632, expanded the country politically and militarily.

Territorial Expansion

Kristina, Gustavus's only child, was six when she inherited the throne. Until she came of age, a group of nobles led by Oxenstierna ran the Swedish government. After 16 more years of fighting, the Thirty Years' War ended with the Peace of Westphalia. This treaty gave Sweden important territories in Germany. As Queen Kristina grew older, she became a patron of artists and scholars. The queen was unable, however, to solve the financial problems the country faced as a result of prolonged warfare. In 1654, having been secretly converted to Catholicism, Kristina gave up her throne and left the country for Rome.

Under Karl X Gustav, Kristina's cousin and successor, Sweden fought Denmark and acquired Skåne, Halland, and other Danish possessions. Sweden also gained control of the Öresund, the main inlet to the Baltic Sea, as well as some parts of Norway. When Sweden and Denmark signed a treaty called the Peace of Roskilde in 1658, Sweden was a great power

Independent Picture Service

Kristina, the only child of Gustavus Adolphus, became a patron of the arts during her reign as queen.

Protestantism and to reinstate the Roman Catholic Church. During this conflict, known as the Thirty Years' War, the Hapsburg armies advanced toward the Baltic, intent on extending the Hapsburg Empire to northern Europe. To meet this threat to Sweden's territory and also to protect Protestantism, Gustavus led an army to Germany. In 1632 the Swedish forces defeated the Hapsburgs at the Battle of Lützen. Although the victory ensured Sweden's independence, Gustavus was killed in the fighting.

in northern Europe. Swedes even founded a short-lived colony on the Delaware River in North America.

Nearly 20 years of peace followed the war with Denmark. That interval allowed the next king, Karl XI, to improve Sweden's trade, defenses, and financial situation. Karl XI also reformed the legal code, the church, and the educational system. At the king's request, the Riksdag reduced the holdings of the nobles, giving much of their land to the crown and to farmers. The monarch also persuaded the Riksdag to pass laws giving him almost unlimited powers.

In 1697, at the age of 15, Karl XII ascended the throne. In 1700 he launched an ambitious military effort in Europe. Karl's motive for the Great Northern Campaign —as the 18-year effort is known—was probably to destroy Russia, a rival power. In the early years, Karl's armies were very successful, advancing steadily into Russia. At the Battle of Poltava in 1709, however, Russia defeated the Swedes and forced them to retreat.

In 1715 Karl XII returned to his homeland for the first time since the campaign began. In 1718, after raising a new army and trying to invade southern Norway, he was shot. After his death, the country gave up most of its lands east of the Baltic and was reduced roughly to the area of present-day Sweden and Finland.

The Era of Liberty

Although the Swedes had admired the heroic qualities of Karl XII, the long years of warfare turned them against the system of unlimited royal authority. After Karl died, a widespread, bloodless revolution resulted in a new constitution that gave basic governmental powers to the Riksdag. One of the monarch's few remaining powers was to appoint the 24 members of the council of advisers. The choices, however, had to be made from a list compiled by the Riksdag. The chancellor, as head of

Independent Picture Service

In the early 1700s, the scholar Carl von Linné (or Carolus Linneaus), a professor of medicine and botany in Uppsala, devised a system for naming and classifying plants and animals. Still used in modern times, his system gave each plant or animal a two-part Latin name.

the council, became the most powerful person in the government.

Under the leadership of Chancellor Arvid Horn, eighteenth-century Sweden recovered quickly from the effects of the war. The country entered a 53-year period now called the Era of Liberty. Sweden's population grew, and its economy prospered as Europe's demand for Sweden's high-quality iron increased. The period also brought substantial cultural and scientific progress to Sweden. Carl von Linné created a system for classifying plants and animals that is still used. Emmanuel Swedenborg made discoveries in anatomy and astronomy, and his writings expressed new philosophical and religious ideas. Anders Celsius perfected the centigrade thermometer, now used throughout the world.

Two political parties—the Hats and the Caps—competed for political power. The

Hats' base of support was among the upper nobility and wealthy merchants, while the Caps attracted farmers, clergy, and lesser aristocrats. The Hats, who wanted war with Russia in order to regain Sweden's lost territory, opposed Chancellor Horn's foreign policies. Horn kept Sweden out of war until he was ousted in 1738. The Hats came to power and restarted the war. Russia defeated the Swedish army in Finland, and in 1743 Sweden had to give up a large part of southeastern Finland to Russia.

Gustav III

For several decades thereafter, rivalry between the Hats and the Caps intensified, and corruption spread through Sweden's political life. Russia and Great Britain—which wanted Sweden to give up its plans to win territory in Europe—tried to buy influence with the Caps. France, which wanted Sweden to expand at the expense of Russia and Denmark, gave money to the Hats. Caught in foreign intrigues and with no strong leader, Sweden was losing its ability to handle its own affairs.

When Gustav III inherited the throne in 1771, Sweden needed a strong monarch once again. Two years of famine, added to decades of political strife, increased the public's desire to return to a more stable system. The new king assembled the Riksdag in 1772 and demanded a return to ancient laws. He then presented a new constitution, which the Riksdag accepted. The document restored many powers to the monarch but still limited others. For Sweden to declare war, for example, the Riksdag's consent was needed.

Gustav III had considerable power, but he believed in justice for the individual. He abolished torture as a criminal punishment

The artist Elias Martin painted this watercolor of Göteborg about 1787. By that time, the city was the leading cultural and commercial center for western Sweden.

An engraving by John Martin Will shows Gustav III receiving surgical aid after assassins stabbed him in 1792. The king died of his wounds two weeks after the attack, probably committed by nobles who opposed the king's growing power.

and introduced freedom of the press. Arts and literature flourished during his reign. A talented and active figure, Gustav III established the Swedish Academy to recognize cultural achievements and wrote many dramatic works himself. In 1789, while conducting a military campaign against Russia, Gustav led another revolution that restored almost complete power to the monarchy. Three years later, however, a group of nobles who opposed rule by such a powerful king assassinated Gustav.

The 1800s

The reign of Gustav III's son, Gustav IV, was in many ways a time of setbacks for Sweden. Gustav IV's main accomplishment was land reform. His policies combined small, inefficient farming plots into larger ones. In foreign affairs, however, the king was unsuccessful. In the early 1800s, the French general Napoleon Bonaparte set out to conquer Europe. Sweden sent forces to support Great Britain—an important

An iron marker dated 1766 defines property boundaries on land in southern Sweden.

31

Karl XIII became king in 1809 after the *Riksdag* (parliament) removed Gustav IV. Gustav had led Sweden into a costly war with Russia that resulted in the loss of Finland.

A statue of Jean Bernadotte, who became King Karl XIV in 1818, is a landmark in Stockholm. Sweden's current monarch is a direct descendant of Karl XIV.

trading partner—against France. While Sweden's attention was directed to that war, Russia took Finland from Sweden.

The Swedish people blamed Gustav IV for the loss of Finland. In 1809 a group of Swedish military officers arrested the king, and the Riksdag adopted a new constitution that sharply limited the monarch's powers. The Riksdag elected Karl XIII, Gustav's brother, as the new king.

Because Karl XIII was old and childless, officials immediately began to search for a ruler to begin a new dynasty. Guided by their desire to regain Finland from Russia, they picked a military leader of proven ability. He was Jean Bernadotte of France, one of Napoleon's generals. Knowing little about Swedish customs or the language, Bernadotte arrived in Sweden in 1810. King Karl XIII adopted Bernadotte, who became Crown Prince Karl Johan.

Sweden's hopes to win back Finland were short lived, however, for Napoleon invaded Pomerania, Sweden's territory in northern Germany. After taking control of this area, Napoleon turned his armies eastward in an attempt to conquer Russia. Because Napoleon had attacked Pomerania, Sweden joined the war against him. The Swedish crown prince led Swedish and Polish troops in battles that helped defeat his former military commander.

Nevertheless, these efforts did not win back Finland. To make up for that loss, Karl Johan decided to take Norway from Denmark. The Swedish army beat the Danes in 1813, and the Treaty of Kiel forced Denmark to give Sweden most of Norway. When Norway refused to recognize the treaty, Sweden quickly defeated Norwegian troops, and in 1814 the Swedish monarch became the ruler of Norway as well. In 1818 Karl Johan was crowned Karl XIV.

For the most part, the governments of Sweden and Norway operated separately. They did share a common foreign policy, but disagreements weakened the union of the two countries. Sweden, where the monarch resided, was the dominant power, and Norway wanted independence.

Although very capable, Karl XIV proved to be a conservative ruler who did not welcome change. Yet in a progressive move, he introduced compulsory education in 1843. His successors enacted more liberal reforms, one of which was a restructuring of the Riksdag. Instead of the traditional four groups—nobility, clergy, burghers, and small landowners—the Riksdag was rearranged to contain two houses. Other reforms of the mid-nineteenth century guaranteed religious freedom and equal rights of inheritance for men and women. Punishments for lawbreakers became less severe.

EMIGRATION AND LABOR

During the 1800s, widespread poverty existed in Sweden. As in other parts of Europe, the birthrate climbed during peacetime. The introduction of potatoes as a food crop and improved health measures also fostered population growth. At times, the number of people grew faster than the country's ability to feed itself.

Sweden's population rose from 2.5 million in 1815 to 3.3 million by 1845 and to 5.1 million by 1900. Poverty forced about 850,000 Swedes to emigrate—mainly to the United States—between 1840 and 1900. Many of these Swedes settled in Minnesota, Illinois, and other parts of the north central United States.

Another change occurred during the same period that had far-reaching consequences for Swedish society. Associations of trade workers and laborers developed in the late 1880s, when less than 10 percent of the population had the right to vote. These labor organizations provided an

Courtesy of House of Emigrants, Växjö, Sweden

This peasant family lived at Aneboda, in southern Sweden, in the late 1800s.

The Swedish scientist Alfred Nobel invented dynamite in 1866. Nobel regretted that the explosive could be used as a weapon, and he later became a pacifist (one who is opposed to warfare). He used his wealth to establish a fund to recognize outstanding individuals who contribute positively to the world. The prizes in literature, medicine, chemistry, physics, and economics are presented annually in Sweden. The Nobel Peace Prize is given each December in Oslo, Norway.

outlet for political expression. The labor movement also emphasized education for workers, and unions established schools and training programs. In the 1890s, many labor groups came together politically under the new Social Democratic party.

INDUSTRIALIZATION

Despite the economic problems of the period, the second half of the nineteenth century brought important industrial advances to Sweden. The invention of dynamite by the Swedish scientist Alfred Nobel allowed passages to be blasted through rocky terrain. Thereafter, the country built many roads and railways. This transportation network, combined with foreign capital, encouraged industrialization.

The development of Swedish manufacturing created jobs and slowed the flow of emigrants from Sweden. Forest industries, including steam-driven sawmills, expanded as other countries stepped up their demand for Swedish lumber. Timber companies harvested the native forests of Norrland.

A steel mill in Munkfors sits beside the Klar River. The mining of iron ore and the production of steel and other iron products have been important to the Swedish economy for centuries. So valued were ironworkers in the 1700s that they received special privileges, including freedom from military service. In the late 1800s, factories in Britain purchased most of Sweden's iron and steel. This changed as Sweden industrialized, and by the twentieth century Swedish factories were using half or more of the ore and iron products.

Photo by Kay Shaw Photography

In the early 1900s, many Swedes left their farms *(left)* to find jobs and housing in Stockholm *(below)* and other cities.

Photo by Kay Shaw Photography

Courtesy of Harlan V. Anderson

Swedes invented new techniques for making wood pulp and paper, for extracting iron from ore, and for making high-quality steel. Other European countries imported great amounts of Sweden's iron and steel. Swedish engineers turned those materials into new industrial products, and factories began producing many consumer goods.

The Early Twentieth Century

Throughout this time of rapid growth, Sweden and Norway remained in the union that was established in 1814. Norway's parliament, however, had become much more powerful, in relation to the king, than Sweden's parliament. This political difference between the two countries made their continued union unworkable. In 1905 Sweden's King Oscar gave up the Norwegian crown, thus peacefully dissolving the union.

Living conditions for most Swedes in the early 1900s were poor. Many families resided in slums in the larger cities. As the state industrialized, living conditions worsened for workers. In 1907 Gustav V responded to the growing pressure for

35

Independent Picture Service   Independent Picture Service

In the 1930s, workers built dams *(left)* on Norrland's rivers to harness power for electricity. High-voltage transmission lines carried the electricity to Stockholm and southern Sweden. The availability of this energy source stimulated many Swedish industries, such as shipbuilding *(right)*.

reforms, and a committee began to study the need for social-welfare legislation.

In 1909 all men over 24 years of age received the right to vote. For the first time, each man's vote counted equally in electing members to one of the two houses of the Riksdag. (Women gained the right to vote in 1919.) With broader representation, Sweden's government became more attentive to solving the country's social problems. In 1913 the government established its first old-age pensions, raised teachers' pay, revised the criminal code, and began to regulate shop hours.

THE WORLD WARS

When World War I (1914–1918) broke out in Europe, Sweden—like Norway and Denmark—declared its neutrality. At first the war stimulated Sweden's industries, which sold goods to the warring nations. Before the conflict ended, however, food was in short supply, and the country was experiencing economic difficulties.

The socialist and labor leader Hjalmar Branting emerged as a strong political figure in the postwar period. Branting supported a gradual and peaceful reform of Swedish society, rather than the immediate change and revolution that some political groups favored. The Swedish economy rebounded rapidly in the early 1920s, and the country became very prosperous.

During the 1930s, however, the nation's economy was hurt by a worldwide economic depression. In response to worsening conditions, voters elected the first Social Democratic government, led by Per Albin Hansson. Supported by workers and farmers in the Riksdag, Hansson enacted welfare measures that improved living conditions.

Before the extensive welfare reforms were in force, however, World War II (1939–1945) broke out in Europe. Sweden again declared its neutrality. Unlike neighboring Denmark and Norway, Sweden was not invaded during the war, which enabled the country to stay out of the conflict. In order to use resources wisely during the war, the state extended its regulation and control of private industry.

As part of its humanitarian efforts, Sweden provided refuge for war victims, including Jews, Norwegians, Danes, Finns, and other peoples living near the Baltic Sea. The Swedish diplomat Raoul Wallenberg is credited with saving 20,000 Hungarian Jews from the Nazi death chambers. After the war, Sweden gave substantial economic aid to Norway and Denmark.

Postwar Changes

Hansson died in 1945, but the Social Democratic government continued under Tage Erlander. Postwar reforms brought about the welfare society that had been planned in the 1930s. New laws provided for a better pension system, payments to families with children, health insurance, housing assistance, and educational reforms. The government enacted steeply graduated income taxes to fund these benefits. Wage earners with the highest incomes were taxed the most heavily. This law caused Sweden to have few wealthy or poor people.

In international politics, Erlander guided Sweden's independent, neutral course while working actively for the cause of world peace. Sweden joined the United Nations in 1946. A Swede, Dag Hammarskjöld, directed that organization as secretary general from 1953 to 1961, when he was killed in a plane crash. In the early 1950s, Sweden joined the Nordic Council, an organization that promotes cooperation among the five Scandinavian countries.

To protect its borders, Sweden built a strong military force but did not participate in the North Atlantic Treaty Organization (NATO)—a defensive alliance of Western nations. Erlander was prime minister, as well as chairman of the Social Democratic party, until 1969, when Olof Palme succeeded him in both posts.

Independent Picture Service

Dag Hammarskjöld, who had served in the Swedish government for 17 years, was appointed secretary general of the United Nations (UN) in 1953. He took part in settling crises in Egypt and Lebanon and sent a UN peacekeeping force to the Belgian Congo (Republic of Congo). He was killed in a plane crash in 1961.

Courtesy of Swedish Embassy

Prime Minister Olof Palme was assassinated in 1986 while walking with his family on a street in Stockholm. His slayer has not been found, and the motive for the killing is unknown.

37

Sweden's major cities grew rapidly in the 1960s, and the nation faced severe housing shortages. Swedes debated the practicality of large, high-rise apartments and the value of smaller, separate dwellings in which residents could be closer to the natural environment. The builders of these apartments in Västerbotten left as many trees as possible undisturbed during construction in the 1970s.

Sweden has a long tradition of freedom of speech, and demonstrations on city streets are common. Popular causes in recent years have been international issues, better environmental protection, and the development — or abandonment — of nuclear energy.

The Viggen is the pride of Sweden's aviation industry and of the Swedish Air Force. In keeping with its policy of neutrality, the nation refuses to participate in any military alliances but keeps an air force for defensive purposes.

Courtesy of Swedish Defense Staff

Recent Events

The early 1970s was a time of economic and political change in Sweden. To gain economic advantages, Sweden and six other nations formed the European Free Trade Association. The organization signed an agreement to cooperate with the European Community (EC) in 1973. During the same period, however, Sweden felt the effects of an international economic recession, caused in part by steep rises in oil prices. Industrial expansion slowed, and unemployment rose.

During this period, significant governmental changes also occurred in Sweden. Proposals that Swedish officials had been studying since the 1950s were implemented. The Riksdag became a single-chamber (unicameral) parliament. A new constitution was adopted in 1974 that took away the monarch's last remaining powers—the right to appoint governmental ministers and to preside over the cabinet. As Sweden's economic problems persisted, however, support for the Social Democrats declined, and in 1976 their long control of the Swedish government ended.

A nonsocialist coalition (group of parties) formed the next government, with Thorbjörn Fälldin, chairman of the Center party, as prime minister. Heated debate arose among Swedish groups over whether more nuclear power plants should be built in their country. The controversy led to the collapse of the Fälldin government in 1978. The next administration, headed by Ola Ullsten of the Liberal party, also resigned over this issue. In a referendum (public vote) in March 1980, the Swedish people decided to expand the number of nuclear reactors to a maximum of 12 but to stop using those power sources by 2010. The problem remained of finding a substitute for these important sources of electricity.

Employment then became a leading political issue. In 1982 the Social Democratic party received a clear majority of votes, and Olof Palme again became prime minister. Palme's policies, combined with a changing international situation, improved Sweden's economy. Just as the country's problems were easing, an unknown attacker assassinated Palme in February 1986. The violence against the well-liked public official shocked the Swedish population. Ingvar Carlsson, also a Social Democrat, succeeded Palme and continued his policies.

By the end of the 1980s, Sweden again faced serious economic problems. With an unemployment rate of only 1.6 percent, labor was in short supply. Yet, on any given day, about 25 percent of Swedish workers stayed home from their jobs. Strikes by the country's strong unions contributed to the absenteeism. Inflation—rapidly rising prices for goods and services—also threatened the nation's economic well-being.

In elections held in 1991, the Conservative party defeated the Social Democrats. Carl Bildt, the leader of the Conservative party, became Sweden's prime minister. Under Bildt, the government has worked to curb Sweden's economic problems by reforming the welfare state. As a result, health benefits will eventually be paid by employers, workers' sickness benefits were reduced to help lessen absenteeism, and some aid to foreign countries was cut. Officials also plan to privatize some Swedish companies in an effort to make the country's industries more competitive in the world market.

Courtesy of Swedish Embassy

Since becoming Sweden's prime minister in 1991, Carl Bildt has concentrated on improving the country's economy.

Photo by Nils-Johan Norenlind, courtesy of Swedish Parliament

The Riksdag, Sweden's unicameral (one-house) legislature, meets in Stockholm. The five main political organizations are the Social Democratic, Moderate, Center, Liberal, and Communist parties. Their members in the Riksdag debate issues and make laws that affect Sweden's 8.9 million citizens.

While on a visit to Washington, D.C., in April 1988, Sweden's King Carl XVI Gustav and Queen Silvia posed in front of the Swedish royal family portrait at the National Portrait Gallery. The couple's eldest child, Princess Victoria *(center)*, is first in line to inherit the Swedish throne. The other children are Carl Philip *(left)* and Madeleine.

Government

Sweden's government is a limited constitutional monarchy with a parliamentary system. Executive authority rests with the cabinet, consisting of a prime minister and 21 other ministers who head government departments. The role of the monarch is formal and symbolic.

The Riksdag is a unicameral parliament with 349 members, who are normally elected by popular vote every four years. Most members are elected from districts, but 39 of the seats are distributed among political parties in proportion to the total vote each party receives. A party that wins at least 4 percent of the national vote gets one or more seats.

The nation's judicial system includes a supreme court, a supreme administrative court, and a labor court, as well as commissions of inquiry, a law council, district courts, and courts of appeal. Ombudsmen (public officials who investigate complaints) oversee the application of laws and check on abuses of authority.

Sweden is divided into 24 counties, which implement central governmental policies at the regional level. A governor appointed by the central government and a council elected by the voters head each county. Counties can collect taxes and are responsible for overseeing education, public transportation, health care, and environmental protection.

The life expectancy for Swedish children is one of the highest in the world. As residents of a welfare state, they receive medical care, education, and many other benefits from the government. Swedish families, regardless of income level, get a government allowance for each child under 16 and for older children who are still in school.

3) The People

With 8.9 million people, Sweden has the largest population of any Scandinavian country. Most Swedes are descended from Germanic peoples who migrated in ancient times to Scandinavia from the south and from areas east of the Baltic Sea. Almost 83 percent of Sweden's population live in urban areas. About half of the people re-side either in the Stockholm region or along the western coast between Malmö and Göteborg.

Swedish—along with Danish, Norwegian, Icelandic, and Faroese—belongs to the North Germanic branch of the Germanic languages. Most Swedes can understand Norwegian and Danish.

Ethnic Characteristics

Sweden's population has become more diverse in recent decades than it was prior to World War II. Since the war ended in 1945, the country has accepted about 600,000 immigrants. Most have come from Finland and other Scandinavian countries. To solve a labor shortage, the country also admitted newcomers from Yugoslavia, Greece, Germany, Turkey, Great Britain, Poland, and Italy.

The government returned to a restrictive immigration policy in the 1970s. Since then, most foreigners accepted for residence—apart from other Scandinavians—have been political refugees, principally

Courtesy of John Rice

The Lapps, or *Sami,* are Sweden's largest minority. The total Sami population throughout northern Scandinavia and Russia is less than 45,000. The people are concerned about preserving their own language, which is spoken in three major dialects, and their traditional culture, including their colorful clothing and decorative handicrafts.

Courtesy of Stan Danielson

Many, but not all, Swedes have blonde hair and blue eyes. For centuries after the country's early settlement by Germanic peoples, no significant immigration into Sweden occurred. Since World War II (1939–1945), however, the population has acquired greater ethnic diversity.

from the Middle East and Asia. A challenge facing the Swedish government is to integrate these new arrivals into Swedish life while preserving their national languages and customs.

Sweden has two minority groups of native inhabitants. About 30,000 Finnish-speaking people live in the northeast along the border with Finland. Scattered throughout northern Sweden and in northern parts of Norway, Finland, and Russia are the *Sami,* or Lapps, whose total population is about 43,000. About 17,000 Lapps make their homes in Sweden. Once a nomadic people who hunted wild reindeer, the Lapps now live in permanent settlements. Many earn their livelihood by breeding and herding reindeer, primarily for meat production. Most Lapps have other occupations as well.

43

Swedish families are small, and most couples limit their families to one or two children. The divorce rate doubled between 1960 and 1980, and one in five couples live together unmarried. The number of women who remain childless is increasing.

Sweden's present rate of population growth is so low that it would take more than 4,000 years for the country's population to double. Unless birth or immigration rates rise, even that growth rate will not be maintained, and Sweden's population could decline. Some Swedes are concerned that as retirees form an ever-larger portion of the population, the country will have difficulty maintaining its current standard of living.

Social Welfare and Health

The Swedish government created the welfare state through careful planning, with constant rethinking and revision to improve it. The numerous governmental programs require considerable record keeping and paperwork, which has resulted in a large bureaucracy.

The national insurance system funds most social-welfare services. Through national insurance, Swedes receive medical and dental care, sickness and parental benefits, and pensions. Other governmental programs provide adult education courses, benefits to injured workers, unemployment payments, general welfare assistance, and allowances to families with children.

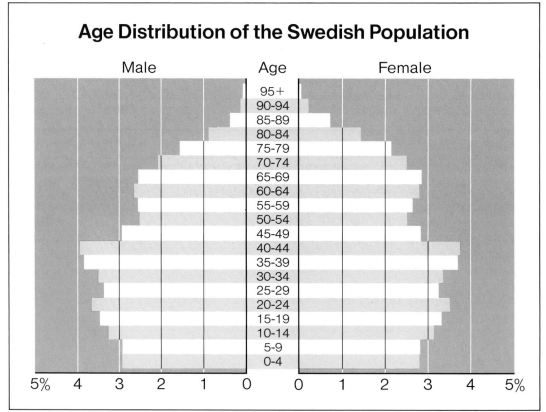

Artwork by Laura Westlund

This population chart shows the age distribution of male and female Swedes in the late 1980s. Changes in the birth and death rates have led to a decline in the percentage of children and to an increase in the proportion of elderly people. Children under 15 make up roughly one-fifth of the population as against one-third 100 years ago. The number of people over 64 has doubled during the past 40 years. (Data provided by the Swedish Institute, Stockholm.)

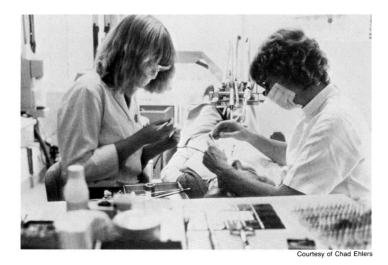

Sweden provides dental care free for children and at low rates for adults. Swedish women are increasingly entering dentistry and other professions that men have traditionally dominated.

Courtesy of Chad Ehlers

One goal of Sweden's welfare administrators is to help older citizens remain in their own homes for as long as possible. This Swede enjoys growing flowers during his retirement years. His house, which is painted red with white trim, is typical of many small dwellings in Sweden.

Courtesy of Swedish Tourist Board

Sweden's commitment to its citizens' welfare begins even before they are born. Partly for that reason, the nation has one of the world's lowest infant mortality rates —4.2 deaths in every 1,000 live births.

An expectant mother gets leave from her job, with pay, one month prior to a child's birth. Parents can divide between themselves an additional 15 months of leave from work, also with pay, after the birth. Although many have waiting lists, public day-care facilities are available when parents return to their jobs, with fees based on the family's earnings. All families, regardless of income, receive an allowance for each child under age 16 and for older children attending school.

Swedes have a high life expectancy—79 years. Many services, including home helpers, have been developed to enable older citizens to remain in their residences and to avoid dependence on institutional care. Retirement housing is available for those who can no longer live in their own homes.

45

Lekvattnet Church serves the religious needs of a parish in Värmland. Most Swedes do not attend worship services regularly, but many choose to have Lutheran ministers perform weddings and funerals.

Religion and Festivals

About 92 percent of the Swedish population belongs to the Church of Sweden, which is part of the Lutheran Church and is the state religion. Since the end of the nineteenth century, free churches—those not connected to the state—have also existed. Among these are the Mission Covenant, the Pentecostalist, and various Baptist churches. Some Swedes who are active in free churches also keep their membership in the Church of Sweden. As a result of immigration after World War II, Sweden also has Roman Catholic and Orthodox churches, Jewish congregations, and small Buddhist and Muslim groups.

Swedish children automatically belong to the state church if their parents are members. To leave the Church of Sweden, citizens must formally withdraw. Less than 5 percent of the population regularly attends church services, but the majority participate in baptism and attend con-firmation classes (religious instruction). Most Swedes also choose to have marriage and funeral ceremonies conducted by the church.

Several of Sweden's largest festivals have religious origins. Christians usher in the Christmas season on December 13 with Santa Lucia Day—the Festival of Light. Before dawn, young girls in white dresses wearing crowns of evergreens and candles wake their families and serve hot coffee and sweet rolls. On Christmas Eve, many families have a traditional dinner that includes *lutefisk*—codfish that has been soaked in lye. The Christmas season extends to Twelfth Night (January 6) or even to St. Knut's Day on January 14.

Early spring brings observances of Lady Day on March 25, which is devoted to the Virgin Mary, and of Easter. A tradition surviving from the pagan religion is the celebration of Walpurgis Eve on April 30. On that occasion, Swedes light bonfires to

Swedes celebrate Santa Lucia Day two weeks before Christmas, when days are very short. The girl chosen to fill the role of Lucia in church and family ceremonies represents the Goddess of Light and the promise of longer days.

Children in Dalarna wear traditional folk costumes while dancing around a maypole. The activity is part of the Midsummer's Eve celebrations that occur throughout Sweden on the Friday between June 19 and 26.

symbolize the sun's return as the hours of daylight begin to increase. Festivities honoring Midsummer's Eve occur on the Friday between June 19 and 26. To celebrate the return of summer, Swedes stay up most of the night and perform traditional dances around brightly decorated maypoles. Flag Day (June 6) is a national holiday.

Education

Swedish children must start school by age seven and complete nine years of compulsory, free education. Kindergarten is not required, although many children attend privately run sessions. English-language study is required from grade three or four.

In the last three years of school, students can select some of the courses they take, and most choose to study an additional foreign language. After completing the compulsory levels, 90 percent of the students go on to upper secondary school for a three-year academic (college preparatory) curriculum or a two-year vocational program.

About 35 percent of secondary-school graduates enroll at a university or professional college, where tuition is free. The government provides study grants and loans for living expenses. Sweden's six universities are in Uppsala, Göteborg, Linköping, Lund, Stockholm, and Umeå. The oldest institution—the University of

Courtesy of Harlan V. Anderson

Passing the final secondary school examination is a high point in the lives of Swedish students who want to attend a university. After the last test, students who have received satisfactory grades emerge from the school wearing white velvet hats *(left)*. This signals their success to friends and relatives, who wait with signs and flowers *(below)*. Families customarily prepare elaborate meals and celebrations to honor the newly graduated young people.

Courtesy of Harlan V. Anderson

These students are studying electronics at a technical school. Almost 85 percent of Swedish youths who finish elementary and middle school continue their education at secondary schools. Many young Swedes wait a year or more before entering high schools, but 95 percent complete that level of education by age 20.

Uppsala—was founded in 1477. Twenty-seven additional facilities also provide advanced schooling. Some of these—in addition to the universities—conduct research and offer postgraduate education. The Karolinska Medical Institute in Stockholm is one of the world's outstanding medical-research centers.

Many Swedes return to school after working for several years. Those who do not pursue formal higher education do not necessarily give up coursework. Thousands of study circles exist throughout the country. Correspondence lessons and adult education programs are also popular. Folk high schools—privately run schools fostered by the labor unions in the late 1800s—offer informal, alternative studies for graduates of the compulsory schools.

Sports and Recreation

Sweden classifies sports into competitive sports, mass-participation sports, and junior sports. Men have dominated competitive sports, but national campaigns have encouraged the increasing participation of women. Soccer is the leading team sport for women, and ice hockey is the

country's most popular team sport for men. Budding athletes can attend sports high schools to combine secondary schooling with physical training. Competitions for disabled men and women have also been developed.

Soccer, which Swedes call *fotboll,* is the most popular organized sport in Sweden. Most soccer players begin receiving instruction in their early years at school. In the compulsory schools, participation in sports is required two or three times each week.

49

Long-distance skiing is one of Sweden's most popular winter sports. The annual *Vasaloppet* (Vasa Race), which covers 54 miles, follows a route taken by Gustav Vasa in 1523 when he was rounding up support to fight the Danes.

In the 1990s, Swedish athletes of international standing included tennis champions Bjorn Borg, Mats Wilander, and Stefan Edberg. Swedish tennis teams have won the Davis Cup—a top international prize—four times. Alpine skier Ingemar Stenmark and high jumper Patrick Sjöberg also achieved international recognition. Sweden has competed well at the Olympic Games, medaling in both summer and winter sports.

Participation in sports for fitness and recreation is a strong tradition in Sweden, where jogging was popular long before it developed into a worldwide trend. Many sporting activities are conducted by 39,000 sports clubs throughout the country. Cross-country and downhill skiing and long-distance skating are popular winter activities. Many Swedes are cycling enthusiasts. Numerous, easily accessible lakes encourage swimming, rowing, and sailing. Increasingly popular with amateur athletes are four annual sports events—the Vasa Race for cross-country skiers, the Vättern Circuit two-day bicycle race,

A trio of cyclers on Gotland find that bikes are a good way to take in the island's historic sites and countryside.

Sweden's many rivers and lakes attract Swedes who like to sail. About one Swedish household in five owns a boat.

the Vansbro Swim, and the Lidingö cross-country run.

Most Swedes spend summer vacations in the country, and many people own rural cottages in abandoned farming areas. The islands near Stockholm are so populated with vacation homes that the area has nearly become an extension of the capital's suburbs. Many Swedes save one week of vacation for a winter ski outing. Although most Swedes spend their time off in Sweden, in recent decades winter trips to resort areas on the Mediterranean Sea and to other areas with mild climates have become popular.

Literature

Modern Swedish literature began with August Strindberg (1849–1912), a social critic whose mocking, satirical writings gained both admirers and critics. The author of 70 plays, Strindberg drew on Sweden's history for his many important dramas and stories. *Master Olof,* Sweden's first great drama, is a psychological study of Gustav Vasa and Vasa's religious adviser. In other works, Strindberg critically examined human society and character. At times mentally ill, the writer described his own disease in two autobiographical works, *The Son of a Servant* and *The Inferno.*

August Strindberg—considered the greatest writer of modern Sweden—wrote plays, novels, short stories, essays, poetry, and autobiographical works. Strindberg experimented with form and dialogue in his plays, which greatly influenced the development of modern drama.

Photo by Kay Shaw Photography

A statue of the writer Selma Lagerlöf sits on the grounds of the large house her family owned near Sunne in the Värmland region.

Independent Picture Service

The actress Greta Garbo attended the Royal Dramatic Academy in Stockholm, the city of her birth. She starred in many Hollywood films.

Selma Lagerlöf, who died in 1940 at age 82, wrote novels and tales about the peasant life of her native district of Värmland, a region rich in folklore. *The Wonderful Adventures of Nils* has become a children's classic. Her celebrated novel *Gosta Berling* was made into a successful film that raised Greta Garbo, its Swedish star, to the top ranks of the film industry. Selma Lagerlöf was the first Swede to win a Nobel Prize.

Vilhelm Moberg, born to a poor farming family in Småland in 1898, chronicled Sweden's past in histories and novels. His three books on Swedish emigration to the United States—*The Emigrants, Unto a New Land,* and *The Last Letter Home*—were made into successful movies.

A writer of a much more philosophical nature was Pär Lagerkvist (1891–1974), a poet and novelist. Lagerkvist won the Nobel Prize in literature in 1951 for *The*

Dwarf and for *Barabbas,* which concerned the sinner in whose place Jesus was crucified. A recurring theme in Lagerkvist's writings is the relationship between God and eternity. In 1974 two Swedish writers—Eyvind Johnson and Harry Martinson—shared the Nobel Prize in literature.

Filmmaking and the Arts

Many Swedish writers tend to be inward-looking, and often despairing. The same tendencies carry over to other areas of cultural expression, including filmmaking. The best-known Swedish filmmaker is Ingmar Bergman, whose works probe the human mind and raise deep philosophical questions. In such films as *The Seventh Seal* and *Wild Strawberries,* Bergman seems to explore the inner person by precisely focusing the camera on the human face. Jan Troell—who adapted Moberg's books in films about Swedish emigrants—and Bo Widerberg are two other prominent Swedish movie directors.

A number of Swedes have achieved international prominence as film actors. Greta Garbo and Ingrid Bergman lead the list. Max von Sydow has starred in a number of Bergman's films. In music, Jenny Lind, "The Swedish Nightingale," was a legend in the 1800s. In the twentieth century, Birgit Nilsson starred in many operas. The Swedish rock group Abba became popular internationally in the late 1970s.

Sweden's greatest visual artists include Carl Larsson, Bruns Liljefors, Gustav Fjaestad and Anders Zorn. All were born in the mid-1800s. Larsson painted many scenes of his own family and home in Dalarna. Liljefors gained international ac-

In the 1800s, many farm families supplemented their incomes in years of poor harvests by making handicrafts. The Dalarna region became famous for its clocks, furniture, metal crafts, and wooden articles—particularly brightly painted wooden horses. Artisans still make toy horses by hand in Dalarna.

claim for his wildlife paintings. Fjaestad loved to depict snow, and Zorn's talents embraced sculpture and portraiture.

Swedish folk arts are as well known to the world as the country's fine arts. A tradition of producing high-quality handmade clothing and utensils developed in the early 1800s. A handicrafts association formed to encourage high standards and to guard against the replacement of Swedish articles by imported goods. Among the finest creations of Swedish craftspeople have been crystal and art glass. In the 1930s, Swedish designers developed a furniture style called Swedish modern—with graceful, functional lines—which proved to have a lasting appeal. Simplicity and beauty became the hallmarks of utensils and objects that Swedes manufactured for everyday use.

The sculptor Carl Milles, who was born in 1875, was one of Sweden's internationally recognized artists. Some of Milles's works are displayed in the garden at his home in Lidingö, a Stockholm suburb. Milles gave the site to Sweden as a museum. In 1929 the sculptor moved to the United States, where he died in 1955.

Courtesy of Stan Danielson

Like other industrialized nations, Sweden has paid a price for its economic development. Pollution from big heating plants, motor vehicles, the pulp and paper industry, iron smelters, and other sources have caused environmental problems. Acid rain, which is caused by air pollution, has damaged one-fifth of Sweden's lakes. This machine is treating a lake to reduce acidification.

4) The Economy

By most measures of living standards, Sweden ranks among the world's top 10 countries. The government works with private companies to maintain full employment. In the late 1990s, the nation had one of the lowest rates of unemployment in the world.

Sweden has accomplished its economic achievements in a short span of time. One hundred years ago, its economy was still largely agricultural. Industrialization be-

gan to take hold in the 1890s. The country experienced worldwide economic downturns —particularly in the 1930s, the early 1970s, and the early 1980s. Yet cooperation among government, labor, and business leaders helped Sweden to recover more rapidly than many nations did.

The Swedish government guides, rather than dictates, how the economy will operate. Ninety percent of businesses are privately owned, and competition exists in most industries. One way the state works with business is by providing placement services and large-scale job-retraining programs. The state assists in the development of new technologies and conducts research that can be applied to specific industries.

Since the 1980s, the government has provided less direct assistance to industries with financial troubles. Public officials have preferred to let competition in the free market determine which companies will survive and which will be phased out.

Agriculture and Forestry

Only 10 percent of Sweden's land can support crops, and for many years the country could not produce enough food to feed its people. Several improvements changed this situation. Small farms gave way to larger holdings on which modern farming techniques are used. With better irrigation methods, higher-yield seed strains, and increased use of fertilizers, Swedish farmers have made the country almost self-sufficient in food. As agricultural output has increased, the farming work force has

The best crop-producing area of Sweden is Skäne, the southernmost region. Only about 10 percent of the country is able to grow crops, although much of the remaining nonforested lands can support livestock.

Most grain planted in Sweden provides feed for livestock. Since 1945, Swedish farms have become larger and fewer in number. Families who own their own land still do most crop farming.

steadily declined and now represents only 3 percent of the Swedish population.

Sweden's growing season varies from 240 days in the south to only 140 days in the far north. Grain and hay can ripen in the north, however, because continuous sunlight in midsummer allows crops to mature in a shorter length of time. The northern river valleys support vegetable farming. A variety of crops grow in the south, including wheat, sugar beets, potatoes, oilseeds, and peas. Farmers in central

Swedish farms raise approximately 1.7 million beef and dairy cattle. Most dairy herds are very small, each averaging about 20 cows.

Forests have long provided the raw materials for Sweden's important paper, pulp, and wood-products industries. Forestry in Sweden is now largely mechanized. The country is a major exporter of pulp products to Europe.

Sweden raise cereals, feed for livestock, and oil-yielding plants.

Much of Sweden's harvest goes to nourish livestock, which produce three-quarters of the country's farm earnings. Swedish farmers raise large numbers of beef and dairy cattle, pigs, reindeers, and sheep. Most poultry operations house several thousand birds. Many farms include a significant amount of forested land. Typically, farmers supplement their income by working part-time in the forestry industry or by selling standing timber to large companies for harvesting.

Using these forest resources, Sweden has become the world's third largest producer of paper and board. Sweden exports the bulk of these products to Great Britain, Germany, and France. The Swedish sawmill industry is the largest in Europe. Most of the lumber is exported to other European countries.

To preserve forestry resources, the government requires forest owners to replant cut areas and to thin woodlots that are too dense. Loggers are trained to protect scenic areas and valuable habitats of flora and fauna. The government estimates that Sweden has more trees now than ever before, thanks to careful management and new plantings.

Conservation through recycling is also practiced, and the pulp industry is collecting increasing amounts of used paper to make into new material. Sixty-six percent of the pulp and paper turned out by Swedish mills is exported. The industry's plants caused serious environmental problems in Sweden prior to the 1970s. Since that time, however, waste discharges into water and the atmosphere have been greatly reduced, and companies have invested heavily in equipment to minimize pollution.

57

Manufacturing and Mining

Sweden's industrial sector, which employs about one-quarter of the nation's 3.9 million workers, is dominated by large companies. Swedish firms are among the world leaders in the use of computer-assisted design and manufacture. Sweden's traditional liberal trading regulations and low tariffs (import taxes) encouraged the growth of foreign trade and Swedish industry. Recently, that growth has slowed. Worker shortages and other labor problems make Swedish companies increasingly reluctant to build new plants in Sweden. Many have opted to construct and expand factories overseas instead.

Companies that develop and manufacture engineered products—including transportation equipment, household appliances, and heavy machinery—make up the largest industrial sector in Sweden. Foreign demand for Swedish-made cars, trucks, and buses increased steadily during the 1980s and early 1990s and was particularly strong in the United States. Swedish automotive manufacturers also produce heavy engines and military and civilian aircraft.

The mining and steel industries have declined in recent years and now employ about 47,000 workers. Yet Sweden remains the world's sixth largest exporter of iron ore, nearly all of which is mined north of the Arctic Circle by a state-owned company. Other sites in northern Sweden provide copper, lead, zinc, silver, gold, and other metals.

Steel production remains important to the economy despite cutbacks. The state and private firms cooperate in the manufacture of commercial steel. Private companies are important world suppliers of stainless and other specialty steels.

The chemical industry—one of Sweden's oldest manufacturing areas—began producing explosives and fertilizers more than a century ago. Chemical and pharmaceutical

Swedish car manufacturers have attempted to humanize the work place by abolishing assembly-line monotony in which a worker performs the same job all day. Managers assign teams to produce large sections of a vehicle. Team members vary the tasks necessary to accomplish their team's job.

Swedes began mining copper at Falun in the late thirteenth century. In time, Falun's large mine became Sweden's single most important source of earnings. The mine continued to yield copper into the twentieth century, but now its metal has been used up. Nevertheless, the company—one of the oldest in the world—pursues other industrial activities.

Scientific research is carried out in private laboratories—such as this one at a pharmaceutical company—as well as at university and other public research facilities in Sweden. The production of chemicals and plastics is an important part of the country's manufacturing sector. The output of pharmaceuticals and biotechnology products has expanded rapidly in recent years.

The Swedish glass industry dates to 1556, when Gustavus Vasa brought skilled glassblowers from Venice, Italy, to Sweden. More than 200 glassworks developed, many of them located in the forests of Småland. In the early 1900s, designers began sculpting crystal and sometimes etched the glass with delicate pictures and symbols. Since then, art crystal has become one of Sweden's most famous products.

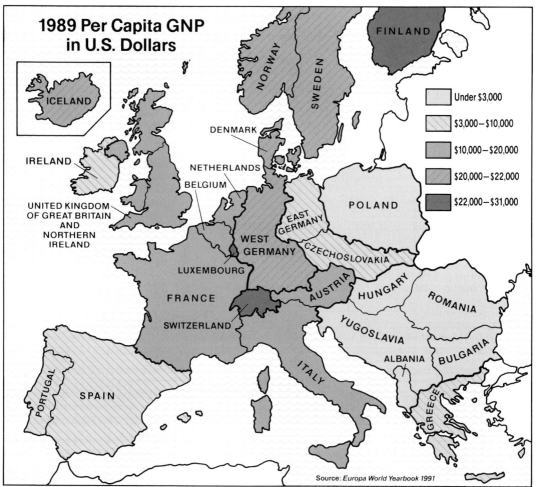

Source: *Europa World Yearbook 1991*

Artwork by Laura Westlund

This map compares the average productivity per person—calculated by gross national product (GNP) per capita—for 26 European nations. The GNP is the value of all goods and services produced by a nation in a year. To arrive at the GNP per capita, each nation's total GNP is divided by its population. The resulting dollar amount is one measure of the standard of living in each country. Sweden's figure of $21,710 meant that in 1989 the country ranked fifth highest in Europe, after Switzerland, Luxembourg, Finland, and Norway.

firms employ about 75,000 Swedish workers. Shipbuilding, another long-established industry in Sweden, has declined in importance. Swedish shipyards no longer build merchant vessels and function primarily as repair sites.

Food processing is an important area of the Swedish economy, with a farmers' cooperative and a consumer cooperative among the biggest food producers. State-owned companies make most alcoholic beverages in Sweden. A number of private firms carry out textile and clothing manufacturing and also account for a large printing and publishing industry.

Trade and Energy

Trade is very important to Sweden's continued prosperity. Sweden belongs to the European Free Trade Association and has had an industrial free-trade agreement with the European Community (EC) since the early 1970s. In 1991 Sweden abandoned its policy of neutrality and applied for full membership in the E.C. The government wants to obtain equality for Swedish companies in the exchange of goods and services and in the movement of investment funds and labor within the EC.

About 20 Swedish corporations that own smaller companies throughout the world dominate Sweden's export industries. Sales of Swedish products abroad increased during most of the 1980s. But by the end of the decade, the government was concerned that high labor costs were making some Swedish goods so expensive that foreign demand would drop. Sweden exports mainly to western Europe and North America. In the early 1990s, more than half of Sweden's exports went to five countries—Germany, Great Britain, the United States, Norway, and Denmark.

Sweden buys most of its imports from Europe and North America. In the early

1990s, Germany was the largest supplier, furnishing at least 20 percent of the goods purchased abroad. Machinery and equipment for use in Sweden's own industries make up the largest share—20 percent—of manufactured imports. Japanese cars are popular in Sweden and account for 30 percent of imported vehicles.

Sweden imports more than half of its energy sources, including all of its oil and most of its coal. Domestic hydroelectric plants and nuclear power plants provide all of the country's electricity and together meet 30 percent of its total energy needs. The Swedish people are concerned about the safety of nuclear plants, however, and voted to close down all such facilities in their country by 2010.

Because of its cold climate and industrial demand, Sweden's energy consumption per person is among the highest in the world. During the international oil crisis

In 1990 hydroelectric installations provided half of Sweden's electricity. The country's energy consumption per capita is among the highest in the world. Heating requirements in the severe climate and an energy-intensive industrial sector contribute to high energy use. Also a factor is the long distances raw materials and finished goods must travel. Sweden's dependence on hydroelectricity will grow, since the country plans to phase out its nuclear plants by 2010.

Sweden's shipbuilding industry has changed its function in recent decades. Former shipbuilders now specialize in the production of equipment such as offshore rigs for the oil industry. This rig was built in Göteborg, one of Sweden's major ports. Sweden produces very little of its own oil and must rely primarily on imports for this energy source.

Courtesy of Göteverken Avendal

of the 1970s, Swedes showed that they could lower energy use significantly through conservation efforts. Industry, too, began to use energy more efficiently during this period.

The Future

Despite its overall success, the Swedish system of government has not solved all the country's social problems. In the late 1980s and early 1990s, job absenteeism rose sharply. On any given day, one out of every four workers stayed away from work. Some social critics say this indicates that Swedes are becoming unhappy with

a society that takes so much of their income in taxes. These critics also observe that the narrow difference in pay between the nation's skilled and unskilled workers discourages Swedes from acquiring new abilities and gives them little incentive to advance.

In the early 1990s, the Swedish government began to address these economic and social issues. Officials drew up plans to reform the welfare state. As a result, many government benefits, including health insurance and pension payments, were reduced.

In 1995, four years after applying for admittance, Sweden was accepted as a full

The colors of the Swedish flag were taken from the country's coat of arms. The flag was first used in the mid-1400s and became the official national emblem in 1663.

member in the EC. Officials hope that increased trade with fellow members of the EC will help boost Sweden's faltering economy.

Whether reform of Sweden's economy and welfare state succeeds will depend on the Swedish people's willingness to adapt to change. Historically, Swedes have shown a firm sense of social concern. This trait gives Swedes the motivation to help their nation meet the challenges of coming years.

Manor houses and castles link modern Swedes to their ancient heritage.

Index